The Hen who laid the Golden Egg

In attempting to gain too much through greed,
All is lost.
It is a sad tale you are about to hear,
That of a family who had a hen
Which every day laid one golden egg.

Because of this her owner decided that
There must be more treasure inside her:
So he killed her, opened her up and found
That she was no different from any other hen!
He had destroyed his one asset out of greed.

La Fontaine

Illustrations by **CARLOS BUSQUETS**
from the original text by **LA FONTAINE**

© LITOR PUBLISHERS LTD – BRIGHTON

This is a lesson for all poor people!
Since time began many such cases have occurred
Of people who become even poorer
Out of the desire to become rich too easily!

The Sponge-carrier and the Salt-carrier

A herdsman was driving his two long-eared donkeys
On a long and arduous journey.
The one loaded with sponges trotted along easily
But the other was dragging his feet;
His load of salt was very heavy.
After much travelling over mountains,
Along valleys and over rough ground,
Our band of travellers, to their dismay,
Finally arrived at the banks of a river.
This is where their problems really began.

The donkey-driver who had often crossed rivers,
Thought he knew it all.
He jumped on the back of the donkey carrying sponges
And herded the tired salt-carrier into the river.
He went into the water,
Right up to his head.
But he was in a dip and soon
Resurfaced and swam on.
In fact the salt was dissolving
And the tired beast felt the weight
Fall from his shoulders.
What a relief!

His companion, on seeing his friend's ease
In crossing the river, followed,
Just like a sheep.
He plunged into the water up to his neck,
All were soaked;
The donkey, the herdsman and the sponges.
The sponges became so saturated
That the weight was too great.
The donkey realised that
He could not reach the other side.

The driver clung onto the animal
Expecting that he would drown very soon.
But someone will save them; though
The method need not be described here.
For the purpose of this fable,
It is enough that our story demonstrates
That it does not do at all
For everyone to act in exactly the same way
In order to achieve the same result.

TITLES IN THE SAME SERIES